TRY NOT TO LAUGH CHALLENGE

EASTER JOKE BOOK
for kids

Easter Jokes

If you're laughing, you're losing!

Try Not to Laugh Challenge!

Rules:

Pick your team, or go one on one.

Sit across from each other & make eye contact.

Take turns reading jokes to each other.

You can make silly faces, funny sound effects, etc.

When your opponent laughs, you get a point!

First team to win 3 points, Wins!

If you're laughing, you're losing!

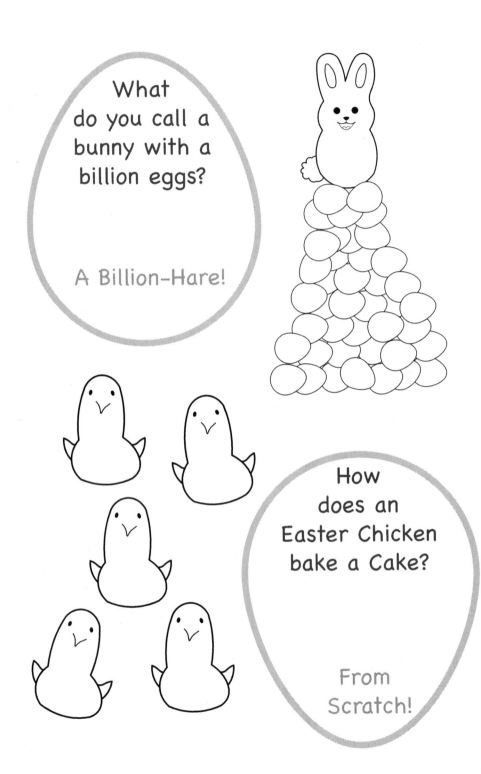

How do you catch a unique bunny?

Unique up on him!

How far can you push a chicken?

Not far, but you can pullet!

Where do you find dinosaur peeps?

Peep-arassic Park!

How does the Easter Bunny stay in shape?

Hare-obics!

What happens if you take someone else's Easter eggs?

You better have a good eggs-planation!

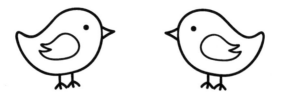

What do you say if the chicks take your Easter candy?

For peeps sake, give me back my candy!

What do you get when you cross the Easter Bunny with a bird?

A Hare-y Woodpecker!

Who is faster, soft or hard boiled eggs?

Soft boiled eggs, because they are always runny!

Why did the Easter Bunny need a library card?

Because he loves to burrow things!

Why did the Easter Bunny throw eggs at the kids?

He wanted to egg them on!

What do you get when you cross a bunny with a cat?

A bunny with hare balls!

Why did the farmer put food dye in his chicken feed?

Because he didn't feel like coloring his own eggs!

What did the old bunny buy when he went bald?

A hare piece!

What kind of music do bunnies like to listen to?

Hip-Hop music!

Knock Knock.
Who's There?
Orange.
Orange you glad it's Spring Vacation!

What do you call a deer that can
paint Easter eggs with his
right and left hoof?

Bambi-dextrous!

What does the Easter Bunny say
when he gets home?

Ear I am!

What time does the rooster crow on
Easter morning?

Eggs-actly 5 o'cluck!

Where does a unicorn go to school?

A Uni-versity!

What is a unicorn's favorite toy?

A Uni-cycle!

Why is a unicorn hard to find?

Because he can be anywhere in the
Uni-verse!

What do you call a unicorn that lives in
the U.S.A.?

Americorn!

What do you get when you put rabbit ears on a Pug?

Easter Puggy!

What did the Easter Egg say to the other Easter Egg?

Have you heard any good yolks lately?

What candy bar is for girls only?

Her-she's

How do you catch baby frogs?

With tadpoles!

What happened to the Easter Bunny when he didn't follow the rules at school?

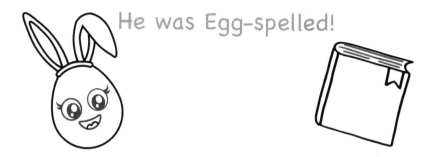

He was Egg-spelled!

Why do all the animals like the Easter Bunny's jokes?

Because his jokes are hare-larious!

Why couldn't the Easter Egg family play their favorite game on their computer?

Because their internet was scrambled!

What do you call a mischievous
Easter Egg?

A practical yolker!

What is invisible and smells like carrots?

A bunny fart!

Where do rabbits learn to fly?

In the hare-force!!

Why did the egg stay at the baseball
game?

Because it had Eggs-tra innings!

How would you send a letter to the Easter Bunny?

By hare mail!

Why don't rabbits get hot in the summer?

Because they have hare conditioning!

Why did the rabbit throw a tantrum?

Because he was hopping mad!

Where does the Easter Bunny eat breakfast?

IHOP!

What does the Easter Bunny wear on his head when he is making Easter Candy?

A hare-net!

What do you get when you cross an elephant with a rabbit?

An rabbit who never forgets to eat his carrots!

Knock Knock.
Who's There?
Midas.
Midas Who?

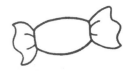

Midas as well start eating our Easter Candy!

What's the difference between a crazy bunny and a fake dollar?

One is bad money and the other is a mad bunny!

Why does the Easter Bunny take so many Selfies?

Because he is Egg-o-centric!

What
do you call a
dumb bunny?

A Hare Brain!

How
long does the
Easter Chicken
work?

They work
around the
Cluck!

Why was the chicken decorated for Easter?

She used to be an Easter Egg!

What happens when the Easter Bunny meets the Bunny of his dreams?

They live Hoppily ever after!

Knock Knock.
Who's There?
Egg.
Egg Who?

Aren't you Egg-cited to see me?

Knock Knock.
Who's There?
Candy.
Candy Who?

Candy the Easter
Bunny carry all
those treats in
one basket?

What does the
Easter Bunny
put on his
boo-boos?

Band-eggs!

What time is it when 5 peeps are chasing you?

5 after 1!

How does the Easter Bunny make Gold Soup?

He adds 14 Carrots!

Why
did the
Easter Bunny go
to the doctor?

He needed an
Eggs-Ray!

Why
do Nesting
Easter Eggs
have no friends?

Because they
are full of
themselves!

Why does the Easter Egg hide?

Because he was a little chicken!

Why did the Easter Bunny fire the Easter Duck?

Because he kept quacking all the eggs!

What did the alien chicks say when
they landed on the earth?

We come in peeps!

Knock Knock.
Who's There?
Anita.
Anita Who?

Anita nother
Chocolate Easter
Egg!

How
does the
Easter Bunny
stay healthy?

He gets lots of
Eggs-ercise!

What do you call a really tired Easter Egg?

Egg-zosted!

Knock Knock.
Who's There?
Chuck.
Chuck Who?

Chuck-olate Bunny!

Why did the Easter Bunny cross the road?

Because the Chicken had his eggs!

Where does the Easter Bunny get his Eggs?

From Eggplants!

How
does the
Easter Bunny
like to travel?

By Hare Plane!

Why
was the
Easter Bunny
upset?

He was having
a bad hare
day!

Knock Knock.
Who's There?
Hedda.
Hedda Who?

Hedda chocolate
egg for you,
but I ate it!

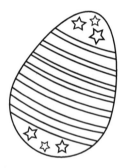

What
day does the
Easter Egg fear
the most?

Fry-Day!

Why don't
Dinosaurs
celebrate
Easter?

Because they
are
Eggs-tinct!

What
did the
Bunny say to
the carrot?

It's been nice
gnawing
you!

How can you tell where the Easter Bunny has been?

Eggs marks the Spot!

What are the Easter Bunny's favorite stories?

The ones with Hoppy endings!

Why did the egg go to school?

To get Egg-ucated!

What is the difference between a unicorn and a carrot?

One is a funny beast and the other one is a bunny feast!

What do you call a line of rabbits walking backwards?

A receding Hare-line!

How do you find the oldest bunnies?

Look for the Gray Hares!

What
do you call
a Bunny with
fleas?

Bugs Bunny!

Knock Knock.
Who's There?
Philip.
Philip Who?

Philip my Easter
Basket with
Candy!

What lives on
the ocean floor
and loves
Easter?

An Oyster egg!

How did the Wet Bunny dry himself?

With a hare dryer!

What do you call a bunny who is really smart?

An Egg-head!

Knock Knock.
Who's There?
Some bunny.
Some bunny who?

Some bunny is
eating all my
candy!

What
kind of
jewelry do
rabbits wear?

14 Carrot
gold!

Where
do you
go to learn
about ducks?

A duck-tionary!

What do you call an egg from outer space?

An Eggs-tra-terrestrial!

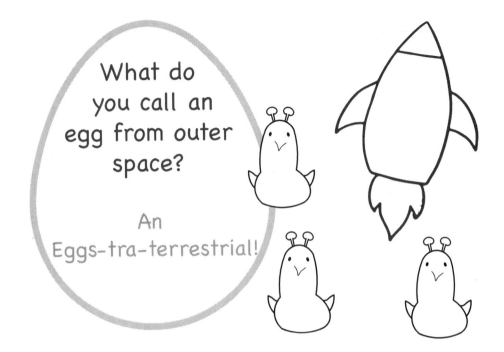

Knock Knock.
Who's There?
Ann.
Ann Who?

An Easter Bunny Butt!

What hangs from a tree at Easter Time?

The Sloth-ster Bunny!

Why is the
letter A like a
flower?

A Bee Comes
after it!

When
does Valentine's
Day come after
Easter?

In the
Dictionary!

What
do you call a
bunny who likes
jokes?

A Funny Bunny!

How
does the
Easter Bunny
keep his fur
looking good?

With
Hare spray!

What happened to the egg after it was told a funny joke?

It cracked up!

Knock Knock.
Who's There?
Arthur.
Arthur Who?

Arthur anymore eggs to decorate?

Knock Knock.
Who's There?
Boo.
Boo Who?

Don't cry,
the Easter Bunny
is coming again
next year!

What
did the
Mommy Egg
say to the baby
egg?

You are eggs-tra
special!

How does the Easter Bunny like to leave the store?

He likes to use the Eggs-it!

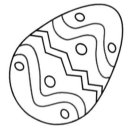

How many Easter Eggs can you put in an empty basket?

Only one, after that it's not empty anymore!

Why did the Chicken take so long to cross the road?

There was no Eggs-Press lane

Knock Knock.
Who's There?
Colin.
Colin Who?

Colin you with some more Easter Bunny jokes!

What do you get when you plant kisses?

Tulips!

What does the Easter Bunny order at a Chinese restaurant?

Hop Suey!

What goes up when the rain goes down?

Umbrella!

Knock Knock.
Who's There?
Donna.
Donna Who?

Donna want to decorate some Easter eggs?

What is a spring chick after it is 5 days old?

6 days old!

What do you get when you cross a bee and a bunny?

A Honey Bunny!

What do you call the door to the chicken coop?

Hen-trance!

Can bees fly in the rain?

Not without their little yellow jackets!

What monster plays the most April Fool's jokes?

 Prankenstein!

How do baby ducks learn to fly?

 They wing it!

Why is everyone so tired on April 1st?

Because they have just finished a long 31 day March!

What do you call a big moose?

Enor-moose!

What season is it when you are
on a trampoline?

 Spring Time!

Knock Knock.
Who's There?
Alma.
Alma Who?

Alma Easter candy is gone! Can I have some
more?

Why are frogs so happy?

They eat whatever bugs them!

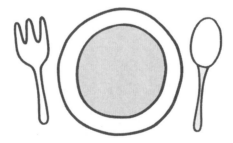

Knock Knock.
Who's There?
Easter.
Easter Who?

Easter anyone home!

What did the baby corn say to the mom corn?

Where's Popcorn?

Why did the Easter Bunny get a ticket?

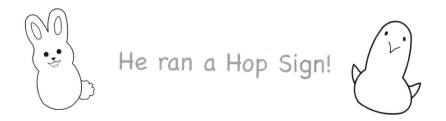

He ran a Hop Sign!

Why did the girl start a gardening business?

Because she wanted to rake in the cash!

Knock Knock.
Who's there?
Imagine.
Imagine who?

Imagine World Peeps!

What's the Easter Bunny's favorite sport?

Basket-ball!

What kind of garden does a baker have?

A "flour" garden!

Where does the Easter Bunny go
on vacation?

Easter Island!

Where do sheep go to get their hair cut?

To the baa-baa shop!

Where do sick bunnies go?

To the Hop-ital!

Knock Knock.
Who's there?
Stella.
Stella who?

Stella nother Easter egg to color!

What did Summer say to the Spring?

Help! I'm going to Fall!

Knock Knock.
Who's there?
Heidi.
Heidi who?

Heidi the eggs around the house!

Knock Knock.
Who's there?
Butcher.
Butcher who?

Butcher eggs in the basket!

How does a pig get to the hospital?

Ham-bulance!

Why did the farmer plant a seed in his pond?

He was trying to grow a
Water-melon!

Knock Knock.
Who's there?
Police who?

Police hurry up and decorate your
Easter eggs!

What time is it when you at a bee's home?

Hive o'clock!

What do sweet potatoes sleep in?

Their yammies!!

What do you call a sheep with no legs?

 A cloud!

How does a rooster say good-bye?

Got to Crow now!

What do bees do with honey?

 They cell it!

Knock Knock.
Who's there?
Wendy who?

Wendy Easter Bunny coming?

Why didn't Beethoven like his chickens?

Because they run around saying Bach,
Bach, Bach, Bach!

Bach!

Why does the duck look forward to the rooster's cock-a-doodle-do?

He likes to get up at the quack of dawn!

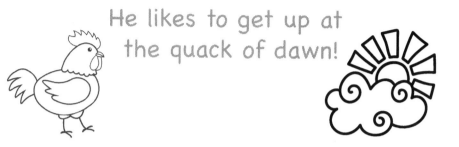

What Easter bird is good at Boxing?

Duck!

What do bunnies like to eat on a hot day?

Hopsicles!

What is the funniest candy bar?

Snickers!

What do you call a frog with no legs?

Un hoppy!

What do you call a horse born on
April Fool's Day?

An April foal!

What is a kangeroo's favorite season?

Spring!

What bow cannot be tied?

A rainbow!

What do you call a bee that talks very softly?

A mumblebee!

Where do newly wed horses stay on their honeymoon?

In the bridal suite!

What chickens crack jokes?

Comedi-hens!

What do you call a cold dog sitting on a rabbit?

A chili dog on a bun!

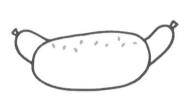 

What leads the duck orchestra?

The con-duck-tor

What duck cracks jokes?

Wise quackers!

Does the Easter Bunny like baseball?

 Yes! He is a rabbit fan!

What is the Easter Bunny's favorite game?

Hopscotch!

What does a lazy rooster say?

Cock-a-doodle-don't!

What does the skunk love to do at school?

Show and Smell!

How do you catch a tame bunny?

Tame way,
unique up on it!

What does the Easter Bunny want to keep in his family?

Hare-looms!

What do you get when you cross a rabbit with a frog?

Bunny ribbits!

Where do you go to learn about chickens?

A Hen-cyclodpedia!

What do you call a happy bunny?

A Hop-timist!

How many apples grow on
an apple tree?

All of them!

Why did the Easter Bunny cross
the road?

To go to the Hopping Mall!

What does the Spanish farmer say
to his chickens?

Oh Lay!

What kind of vegetable is very cool?

A Rad-ish!

What do you have to break first
before you can use it?

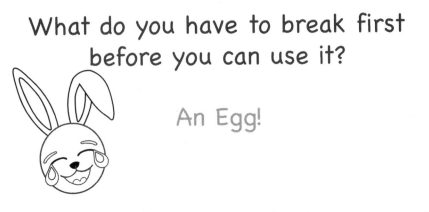

An Egg!

Why couldn't the hen find her eggs?

She mis-laid them!

What has 4 legs, a long body and goes
quack-quack?

A ducks-hund!

What is a tree's favorite drink?

Root Beer!

What medicine do Bumble Bees take when they get sick?

Antibeeotics!

What did the Easter Bunny say to the chicks?

Power to the Peep-le!

What is Beethoven's favorite fruit?

Ba Ba Ba Ba nannas!

Why was the father egg so strict?

He was hard boiled!

Why doesn't bread like warm weather?

Because things get toasty!

What do you call a bird bath on a cold morning?

A brrrrrd bath!

What do you call a Dinosaur at Easter?

A Bunnysaurus!

What did the chick say to his
best friend?

You and I are like two peeps in a pod!

Why do bees hum?

Because they can't remember the
words!

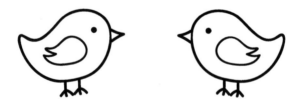

What did one chick say to the
other chick?

Our friendship is growing in peeps and
bounds!

What do you get lots of when it rains
cats and dogs?

Poodles!

What do you get when you cross a cute
bear and a skunk?

Winnie the Pew!

How do deer start a race?

Ready Set Doe!

Why didn't the egg cross the road?

Because he wasn't a chicken yet!

What do you call a mushroom who tells funny jokes?

What a fungi!

What do you get when you cross a Dinosaur and the Easter Bunny?

The Easter Barney!

Knock Knock.
Who's There?
Nose.
Nose who?
I nose where your Easter basket is!

Knock Knock.
Who's There?
Brett.
Brett who?
Brett you don't know where your
Easter basket is!

Knock Knock.
Who's There?
Ashley.
Ashley who?
Ashley maybe I don't know where your
Easter basket is!

Where do you find the biggest eggs
in the U.S.?

Teggs-as

How does the pirate Easter Bunny
hide his treasure?

Eggs marks the spot!

Why doesn't the Easter Bunny like
scary movies?

Because it's a hare raising experience!

What did the Easter Bunny say
to the carrot patch?

I'd like to get to gnaw you!

What do you get when you cross a unicorn with a bunny?

A Bunni-corn!

What do you call a single ear of corn?

A unicorn!

What do you call a cup of pink coffee with whipped cream and a straw?

A uni-frap!

What do you get when you cross a unicorn with a cat?

A kitti-corn!

Why are bunnies so lucky?

Because they have 4 rabbit feet
with them all the time!

Why do you crack your Easter eggs
on the stove on Friday?

Because it's Good Fryday!

Why does the Easter Bunny try to
be good all the time?

Because he doesn't like harey
situations!

What kind of jewelry does the Easter
Bunny like?

Anything with karats!

What game can't you play with a
unicorn?

Leap Frog!

Why are unicorn jokes funny?

Because they are so corny!

What is a unicorn's favorite color?

Rainbow!

What do you call a unicorn with
no horn?

A horse!

How does the Easter Bunny eat
his chinese food?

With hop-sticks!

What do you do if your house is infested
with Easter eggs?

Call the Eggs-terminator!

Why do we paint our Easter eggs?

It is alot easier than trying to
wallpaper them!

What kind of music do bunnies like
to dance to?

The Bunny Hop!

How do you know carrots are good for your eyes?

Have you ever seen a rabbit with glasses?

How is Easter like hot fudge?

They are always on a Sundae!

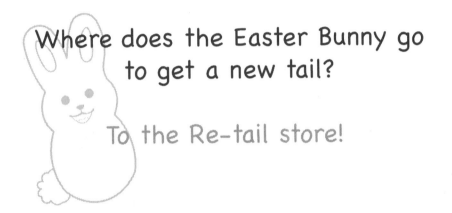

Where does the Easter Bunny go
to get a new tail?

To the Re-tail store!

Why did the student worry that the
Easter Bunny may not find him?

Because he was an
Eggs-change student!

What do ducks have for lunch?

Soup and quackers!

What is the Easter Bunny's favorite dessert?

Carrot cake!

What do Jesus and Bread have in common?

You celebrate when they rise!

Why can't scrambled eggs ever win anything?

Because they are always beaten!

Why did the Easter Bunny laugh at the owl's jokes?

Because the owl was a hoot!

Where do you learn about ancient Easter Bunny history?

At the Eggs-cavation site!

Who tells jokes and changes colors?

A stand up Chameleon!

What did the parrot say when he saw the duck?

Polly wants a quacker!

Why can't you trust a peacock?

They are always spreading tails!

Knock Knock.
Who's There?
Harvey.
Harvey who?
Harvey having fun yet?

Knock Knock.
Who's There?
Iguana.
Iguana who?
Iguana eat more Easter candy!

Knock Knock.
Who's There?
Lettuce.
Lettuce who?
Lettuce all have a Happy Easter!

Knock Knock.
Who's There?
Peeps.
Peeps who?
Peeps on Earth!

What did the chick say to the other chicks?

I like hanging with my peeps!

Who floats down to the ground with an umbrella?

Mary Peepins!

What is the Easter Bunny's favorite video game?

Peepman!

Knock Knock.
Who's There?
Peeps.
Peeps who?
Peeps be with you!

What do you get when you cross a
chick with a pig?

Peppa Peep!

Who is off to see the wizard?

The Peeps of Oz!

Who fell down a hole in the ground and
met a funny rabbit?

Alice in Peepland!

What is the Easter frog's favorite
spring flower?

Croak-us!

What is the safest cat to have?

A dandy-lion!

Why did the chicks get in trouble?

They were using fowl language!

Where is a pig's favorite nap place?

In a ham-mick!

What kind of bunny is always late?

A Choco-late bunny!

What kind of beans will never be served for dinner?

Jelly beans!

What food do deers like the most?

Doe-nuts!

Why was the deer playing in the storm?

Because he was a rain-deer!

Knock Knock.
Who's There?
Nana.
Nana who?
It's Nana your business where my
Easter candy is!

Knock Knock.
Who's There?
Nadya.
Nadya who?
Nadya your head if you want
another chocolate Easter egg!

Knock Knock.
Who's There?
Oink oink.
Oink oink who?
Are you the Easter pig?!

What do you get when you cross a bunny with lemons?

You get hare in your lemonade!

Why does the Easter Bunny fall asleep when he visits the pig?

Because the pig is a boar!

What did the dog cook the Easter Bunny for breakfast?

Pooched eggs!

What kind of dinner did the sheep make for the Easter Bunny?

A Bah-bah-cue!

Knock Knock.
Who's There?
Philippa.
Philippa who?
Philippa my Easter basket again!

Knock Knock.
Who's There?
Queen.
Queen who?
Queen your room and you can have
more Easter candy!

Knock Knock.
Who's There?
Schick.
Schick who?
I am Schick as a dog from eating too
much Easter candy!

Knock Knock.
Who's There?
Freddie.
Freddie who?
Freddie or not, here comes the
Easter Bunny!

Knock Knock.
Who's There?
Gus.
Gus who?
Gus that's what you are supposed
to do!

Knock Knock.
Who's There?
Butter.
Butter who?
You butter get ready for the
Easter egg hunt!

Knock Knock.
Who's There?
Quacker.
Quacker who?
Quaker nother joke to see if you can
make me laugh!

Knock Knock.
Who's There?
Sarah.
Sarah who?
Sarah anymore Easter candy?!

Knock Knock.
Who's There?
Venice.
Venice who?
Venice it your last joke?!

Why does the rabbit bring toilet paper to the party?

Because he can be a party pooper!

Knock Knock.
Who's There?
Wayne.
Wayne who?
The Wayne is coming down so hard
they cancelled the egg hunt!

Knock Knock.
Who's There?
Norway.
Norway who?
There is Norway I am sharing my
Easter candy !

Knock Knock.
Who's There?
Les.
Les who?
Les go look for more Easter eggs!

Knock Knock.
Who's There?
Yule.
Yule who?
Yule be sorry if you eat all your candy at once!

Knock Knock.
Who's There?
Athena.
Athena who?
Athena the Easter Bunny!

Knock Knock.
Who's There?
Buck Buck.
Buck Buck who?
Buck Buck, I'm the Easter Chicken!

Knock Knock.
Who's There?
Canoe.
Canoe who?
Canoe please help me find my last
Easter egg?!

Knock Knock.
Who's There?
Dishes.
Dishes who?
Dishes the last time I will put on these
bunny ears!

Knock Knock.
Who's There?
Emerson.
Emerson who?
Emerson nice bunny ears you
are wearing!

Knock Knock.
Who's There?
Alda.
Alda who?
Alda kids love the Easter Bunny!

Knock Knock.
Who's There?
Juno.
Juno who?
Juno what the Easter Bunny will bring you?!

Knock Knock.
Who's There?
Radio.
Radio who?
Radio or not, here comes the another Easter joke!

Knock Knock.
Who's There?
Gladys.
Gladys who?
Aren't you Gladys it's Easter time?!

Knock Knock.
Who's There?
Duncan.
Duncan who?
Duncan strawberries in chocolate
is fun!

Knock Knock.
Who's There?
Pastor.
Pastor who?
Pastor the Easter ham, I'm hungry!

Knock Knock.
Who's There?
Samantha.
Samantha who?
Can you give me Samantha about
the Easter Bunny?!

Knock Knock.
Who's There?
Cameron.
Cameron who?
Is the Cameron, I want to take
a picture of our Easter eggs!

Knock Knock.
Who's There?
Ada.
Ada who?
I Ada lot of Easter candy and now
I have a stomach ache!

Knock Knock.
Who's There?
Dewey.
Dewey who?
Do we have to share our Easter candy?!

Knock Knock.
Who's There?
Gary.
Gary who?
Gary my Easter basket for me!

Knock Knock.
Who's There?
Alaska.
Alaska who?
Alaska you one more time, why did you eat my Easter candy!

Knock Knock.
Who's There?
Wyatt.
Wyatt who?
Wyatt taking you so long to find your
Easter basket?!

Knock Knock.
Who's There?
Whale.
Whale who?
Whale you decorate my Easter
egg for me?

Knock Knock.
Who's There?
Yeti.
Yeti who?
Yeti nother Easter joke!

Which side of the chicken has more feathers?

The outside!

Why did the bunny go to the hospital?

It needed a hop-eration!

Why did the chicks want a library card?

They wanted to look for bookworms!

How did the bee get out of time-out?

It was on it's best bee-havior!

Why is Sunday the most powerful day?

All the other days are weak days!

Who wants Peace on Earth at Easter?

The Easter Ribbit!

What is long, fun to watch and has lots of cats?

An Easter Purrade!

What two states does the Easter Duck
like to visit?

North and South Duck-ota!

What type of movie do you watch if you
want to learn about the Easter Duck?

An Easter Duckumentary!

What do you call a magical Easter Bunny?

A Mag-Egg-cal Bunnycorn!

© 2018 Howling Moon Press